Wok

Neither saucepan nor frying pan

If I could take only one cooking pan with me to a
desert island, it would be a wok. No modern utensil
can be used in so many ways as the ancient wok.
It is neither saucepan nor frying pan, but you
can use it for almost any kind of cooking.

Whether used for cooking decoratively chopped
fresh vegetables, tender meat, fish or seafood,
it ensures that they all keep their firm texture and,
combined with exotic sauces, spices and other
ingredients, taste absolutely delicious.

What is more, wok cooking is quick. Try this
'wonder pan' with its lovely shape for yourself!
You will never want to use an ordinary pan again.

AURA

CONTENTS

The wok – so ancient, so modern

Two millennia ago when our era began, China was already a highly developed civilization, a state of diverse people with about 60 million inhabitants. It was difficult to rule and suffered frequent natural disasters resulting in famine.

In contrast to the feudal nobility, the poor country people had to make the best of what was left over from tax collectors and bad harvests. Above all, they had to use as little fuel as possible because, even at the best of times, it was always in short supply. The simple Chinese kitchen had an open fireplace or a kind of cooking range, a bench with round holes cut out of it to support pots placed directly over the open fire. The round base of the wok – that successful cross between a saucepan and frying pan – is ideally suited to this kind of cooking. Even in Europe, you can still occasionally find little Chinese restaurants with this kind of fireplace, although most of them prefer the more easily regulated, modern gas hob. Modern woks can also be used on an electric cooker, but the outer base of the wok must be flattened. Even then, the inner base is rounded up towards the high outer rim.

This is what distinguishes the wok from other cooking pans. First, the food to be cooked comes into contact with the hot wok base, which quickly seals it. Then with continual stirring and turning, it is tossed against the sides of the wok, which are slightly less hot so it cooks more gently, until it falls back down to the base again. This method makes for quick cooking, which limits damage to vitamins and other nutrients. At the same time it cooks the food, retaining both texture and flavour.

Preparation and cooking

The classic cooking method for Chinese and many other Asian dishes is stir-frying. It originated as a result of the need to save precious fuel and also through the great respect paid to all foodstuffs, to ensure that they would not lose their own particular taste. Both these objectives can be attained only by cooking for as short a time as possible. This also means that all the ingredients must be cleaned, prepared and cut up into very small, even-size pieces before you begin cooking. Mixed spices and sauces must also be prepared in advance. Only then can you turn to the wok. It should always be thoroughly preheated before you pour in the oil or other cooking fat and begin cooking.

Decoratively chopped ingredients and crunchy fresh vegetables are the basis for delicious stir-fried dishes to be cooked in the wok.

Stir-frying

For the ingredients to keep their colour, flavour and 'bite', they must be cooked in the right order. As a general rule, you begin with the meat or coarser vegetables, such as carrots and cabbage. Food that is cooked is then pushed to the sides of the wok to keep it warm. Larger pieces of meat or vegetables can also be laid to drain on a rack clipped to the rim of the wok. Add the more delicate ingredients next, such as peas, spinach and beansprouts. Lastly, add the spicy sauces or cooking liquid and the other flavourings and thoroughly mix everything together in the base of the wok.

For stirring and turning you can use a wooden spatula or a wok scoop with a rounded front edge, sometimes supplied with the wok. Best of all, use long chopsticks once you have mastered the art of holding and moving the food with them.

Steaming

A particularly gentle cooking method is steaming. Many woks are supplied with a trivet that rests inside it about 3 cm/1¼ inches above the base. It may be made of metal, wood or bamboo. Boiling liquid fills the base below and food can be placed on a plate or in a flat-bottomed bowl on the trivet. Alternatively, the food can be laid directly on it, but should not come into direct contact with the liquid. Then cover the wok with its high rounded lid, so that the rising steam can circulate well.

You can also buy special Chinese steamers, which stand over the boiling liquid, resting against the sides of the wok, and are covered with their own bamboo lids. They are inexpensive and a wide range of sizes is available from most Chinese supermarkets.

Deep-frying

The wok is also excellent for deep-frying. Its wide shape makes it ideal for moving and turning the food to be fried, so that it browns evenly all over. Typically in Chinese and Asian cooking, the fish or meat is marinated in a spicy or aromatic sauce first. Very often the food is dipped in cornflour or batter before frying. If a particularly crisp coating is required, the food must be fried several times. The cooked food can then be laid on the clip-on draining rack or drained on kitchen paper and kept warm.

Wok frying is most enjoyable if you do it at the table with your family or guests assembled. Place all the ingredients beside the wok, including your favourite sauces, in which the cooked food can be dipped. Whether you are frying, stir-frying or steaming the food, cooking it at the table is, of course, only possible if you have an electrically-heated wok or a powerful movable hotplate. Gathering the family together in the kitchen can be almost as much fun.

Other techniques

Of course, you can use the wok for braising and boiling in the conventional way. The way it distributes the heat evenly is a great advantage. Perhaps it is not so well known, however, that the wok is excellent for smoking food – with delicious results. Before you do this, line the wok with extra strong aluminium foil or it will be very hard work to clean it.

Before using it for smoking food, it is essential to line your wok with extra-strong aluminium foil.

When you have finished, you can simply take out the dirty foil and throw it away. If you want to take extra care, you can also protect the lid in the same way.

Sprinkle a handful of whatever you are using for smoking in the base of the wok. You can use juniper berries, allspice berries, cumin seeds, coriander seeds, aniseed, black tea, jasmine tea or dried orange peel. Fit the lid on loosely so that a small gap remains open. Heat the wok over a high heat until you notice the smell of smoke. Lay the food to be smoked – duck breast, chicken legs, whole or filleted salmon – on the trivet and put it into the wok. Now shut the lid tightly and either turn down the heat to medium or remove the wok from the heat, depending on the delicacy of the food. The time it takes to smoke the food depends on what it is and how much it weighs, and on whether you want to smoke it ready for eating or are going to cook it further in some other way.

Materials and accessories

The 'classic' wok, the correct name of which is *kuo*, is made of iron. It heats up quicker and more evenly than any other type, but it can easily go rusty. To prevent this, every time it is cleaned it should be thinly coated with oil. Never clean it with scouring powder or steel wool. It is best to remove any cooked-on food with a wok brush made of split bamboo sticks or a non-metallic saucepan scourer. Then wash it out with hot water and washing up liquid, rinse and dry well. Finally, warm it slightly to make sure it is really dry, and wipe the inside with kitchen paper dipped in oil, but be careful not to burn your fingers! When you use it next, wipe it out again beforehand with oily kitchen paper. Of course, before you use it for the first time you must wash it thoroughly with hot water and washing up liquid to remove the manufacturer's protective coating and then oil it thoroughly to season.

You must also do this with a cast iron wok. You may even need to wash, dry and oil it several times to make sure it is properly seasoned. After they have been seasoned, cast iron woks must be washed using only hot water without detergent.

Cleaning is less complicated with woks made out of more expensive materials. You can use water, washing up liquid and a sponge. You can buy woks made of stainless steel, enamelled steel, cast aluminium, copper and even fireproof china. Some suppliers even offer them with a non-stick coating. The material determines the price. The cheapest is plain iron and the most expensive is the copper wok. Note that non-stick woks cannot be heated to the same very high temperatures as those made of other materials.

You can buy woks with their own electric heater or spirit burner, which is useful when you want to cook companionably at the table.

The original wok has a round base. To cook with it on a gas hob, you will need a stand to keep it steady. Stands are made of metal and may simply be open-sided frames or solid rings with holes punched at regular intervals. Many of the more expensive woks today have a flat bottom, so that you can also cook on an electric hotplate with them. A wok stand is essential for safety when you are using the wok for deep-frying, steaming or braising.

Sometimes woks are supplied with a lid, but not invariably. Lids are dome shaped, tight-fitting and usually made of aluminium. They can be bought separately and are necessary for braising and steaming.

The wok is quite often supplied with a clip-on draining rack. However, it does not necessarily come with a trivet, wok scoop, strainer or ladle. You do not have to have these, but they are very useful, as too are extra-long chopsticks.

Woks are made from a wide variety of different materials. It is sensible to buy the best-quality and heaviest wok you can afford, but do not forget the accessories.

Chicken legs with Chinese cabbage

For beginners • Rather time-consuming

Serves 4
4 chicken legs
  (each about 200 g/7 oz)
salt
Chinese five-spice powder
120 ml/4 fl oz groundnut oil
250 ml/8 fl oz chicken stock
45 ml/3 tablespoons soy sauce
10 ml/2 teaspoons sugar
45 ml/3 tablespoons dry sherry
4 young carrots
4 spring onions
800 g/1¾ lb Chinese cabbage
5 ml/1 teaspoon cornflour
30 ml/2 tbsp water
2.5 ml/½ teaspoon ground coriander

Approximately per portion:
1,630 kj/390 kcal
46 g protein
13 g fat
19 g carbohydrate

● Approximate preparation
time: 30 minutes

---

1. Rub the chicken legs all over with salt and a little Chinese five-spice powder.

2. Heat the groundnut oil in a preheated wok until it smokes. Add the chicken and fry, turning frequently, for 10 minutes.

3. Stir together the chicken stock, soy sauce, sugar and sherry. Pour off the oil from the wok and add the chicken stock mixture. Bring to the boil and braise the chicken legs for about 10 minutes, until the liquid has reduced by about one third.

4. Meanwhile, thinly slice the carrots and spring onions. Shred the Chinese cabbage.

5. Remove the chicken from the wok and keep warm. Add the vegetables to the wok and cook, stirring frequently, briefly.

6. Stir together the cornflour and the water to make a smooth paste. Stir the cornflour paste into the vegetable mixture and cook, stirring constantly, until thickened. Season with salt and stir in the coriander. Place the chicken on the vegetables and heat through. Transfer the vegetables to a serving dish, top with the chicken legs, pour over the sauce and serve immediately.

Chicken with walnuts

Easy to make • Quick

Serves 4
500 g/1¼ lb boneless chicken
  breasts, skinned
10 ml/2 teaspoons cornflour
1 egg white
2.5 ml/½ teaspoon sugar
45–60 ml/3–4 tablespoons dark
  soy sauce
cayenne pepper
4 spring onions
200 g/7 oz mushrooms
½ bunch fresh flat leaf parsley
60 ml/4 tablespoons groundnut oil
90 g/3½ oz shelled walnuts
150 g/5 oz sugar-snap peas
60 ml/4 tablespoons dry white wine
60 ml/4 tablespoons chicken stock

Approximately per portion:
1,900 kj/455 kcal
37 g protein • 32 g fat
14 g carbohydrate

● Approximate preparation
time: 35 minutes

---

1. Cut the chicken into strips and put in a dish. Mix the cornflour with the egg white, sugar, 30 ml/ 2 tablespoons of the soy sauce and season well with cayenne pepper. Pour over the chicken, turning to coat, and set aside to marinate for about 15 minutes.

2. Thinly slice the spring onions and mushrooms. Finely chop the fresh parsley.

3. Heat the groundnut oil in a preheated wok. Add the walnuts and stir-fry for about 30 seconds. Remove the walnuts with a slotted spoon and set aside.

4. Add the chicken, together with the marinade and stir-fry for about 1 minute. Add the vegetables and stir-fry for about 30 seconds. Add the wine and the chicken stock and braise for about 2 minutes.

5. Return the walnuts to the wok, stir in the remaining soy sauce and season to taste with cayenne pepper. Transfer to a serving dish, sprinkle over the chopped parsley and serve immediately.

Above: Chicken legs with Chinese cabbage
Below: Chicken with walnuts

Sweet-and-sour chicken

Rather time-consuming

Serves 4
*500 g/1¼ lb boneless chicken
   breasts, skinned
1 egg white
salt
15 ml/1 tablespoon Chinese rice
   wine or dry sherry
30 ml/2 tablespoons cornflour
2 cm/¾ inch piece fresh root ginger
2 shallots
2 garlic cloves
1 small green pepper
200 g/7 oz can bamboo shoots
350 ml/12 fl oz groundnut oil
30–45 ml/2–3 tablespoons dark
   soy sauce
15–20 ml/3–4 teaspoons rice or
   apple vinegar
5–10 ml/1–2 teaspoons sugar*

Approximately per portion:
1,340 kj/320 kcal
32 g protein
8 g fat
30 g carbohydrate
● Approximate preparation   time: 35 minutes

1. Cut the chicken breasts into bite-size pieces.

2. Beat the egg white with a pinch of salt until it forms soft peaks. Fold in the rice wine or sherry and the cornflour. Stir in the chicken and set aside for about 20 minutes.

3. Meanwhile, finely chop the ginger. Finely dice the shallots. Finely chop the garlic.

4. Seed, core and finely chop the green pepper. Drain the bamboo shoots and cut into thin strips.

5. Reserve 30 ml/2 tablespoons of the oil and heat the remainder in a preheated wok. Add the chicken and stir-fry until browned all over. Remove the chicken from the wok and pour off the oil.

6. Heat the remaining oil in the wok. Add the vegetables and stir-fry for about 1 minute. Return the chicken to the wok and warm through. Stir in soy sauce, rice or apple vinegar and sugar to taste. Transfer to a serving dish and serve immediately.

Mango chicken

Easy to make

Serves 4
*1 kg/2¼ lb chicken
salt
40 g/1½ oz clarified butter
1 fresh mango
4 spring onions
1 lemon
200 ml/7 fl oz chicken stock
freshly ground white pepper
freshly grated nutmeg
mild paprika
75 ml/5 tablespoons crème fraîche*

Approximately per portion:
2,400 kj/570 kcal
27 g protein
35 g fat
6 g carbohydrate
● Approximate preparation   time: 25 minutes

1. Cut the legs and wings off the chicken. Cut the body in half and divide each half into two pieces. Rinse the chicken pieces and rub them with salt.

2. Heat half the clarified butter in a preheated wok. Add the chicken pieces and fry, turning frequently, for about 10 minutes. Set aside and keep warm.

3. Peel, stone and dice the mango. Thinly slice the spring onions diagonally. Grate the lemon rind and squeeze out the juice.

4. Heat the remaining clarified butter in the wok. Add the mango, spring onions and lemon rind and stir-fry for about 2 minutes.

5. Return the chicken to the wok, add the chicken stock and a little lemon juice and bring to the boil. Boil over a high heat for about 5–10 minutes. Season to taste with white pepper, nutmeg and paprika and stir in the crème fraîche. Transfer to a warm serving dish and serve immediately.

Above: Sweet-and-sour chicken
Below: Mango chicken

Chicken with shiitake mushrooms

Rather expensive

Serves 4
600 g/1 lb 5 oz boneless chicken
  breasts, skinned
400 g/14 oz shiitake mushrooms
3 cm/1¼ inch piece fresh
  root ginger
3 shallots
1 garlic clove
105 ml/7 tablespoons chicken stock
45 ml/3 tablespoons Chinese rice
  wine or dry sherry
45 ml/3 tablespoons light soy sauce
½ bunch chives
10 ml/2 teaspoons cornflour
5–10 ml/1–2 teaspoons clear honey
salt
boiled rice, to serve

Approximately per portion:
1,200 kj/290 kcal
45 g protein
4 g fat
14 g carbohydrate

● Approximate preparation
  time: 45 minutes

---

1. Cut the chicken breasts into bite-size pieces. Trim the mushroom stalks and thinly slice the mushrooms.

2. Thinly slice the root ginger. Cut the shallots into quarters and cut the garlic in half.

3. Fit the trivet in the wok and pour in sufficient boiling water to reach just below it. Stand a wide heatproof dish on the trivet.

4. Put the chicken, together with the mushrooms and chicken stock, into the dish and sprinkle over 30 ml/2 tablespoons of the rice wine or sherry and 30 ml/2 tablespoons of the soy sauce. Add the ginger, shallots and garlic and cover the wok.

5. Steam for about 15–20 minutes, until you can smell a pleasant savoury aroma. Meanwhile, snip the chives into pieces about 1 cm/½ inch long.

6. Remove the ginger, shallots and garlic from the wok and discard. With a slotted spoon, remove the chicken and mushrooms from the dish and keep warm. Strain and reserve the cooking liquid. Pour off the boiling water from the wok.

7. Pour the cooking liquid into the wok and bring to the boil. Stir in the remaining Chinese rice wine or sherry and the remaining soy sauce. Stir in the cornflour and bring back to the boil, stirring constantly, until thickened.

8. Stir in 5 ml/1 teaspoon of the honey. If necessary, season to taste with a little salt and add the remaining honey.

9. Return the chicken and mushrooms to the wok and heat through, stirring constantly to coat thoroughly with the sauce. Transfer to a warm serving dish, sprinkle over the chives and serve immediately with boiled rice.

Chicken with shiitake mushrooms acquires a delicious flavour when it is steamed in the wok.

Honeyed duck

Delicious • For beginners

Serves 4
4 boneless duck breasts (each about
* 150 g/5 oz)*
45 ml/3 tablespoons clear honey
45 ml/3 tablespoons hot water
30 ml/2 tablespoons tomato ketchup
5 ml/1 teaspoon Worcestershire
* sauce*
30 ml/2 tablespoons dark soy sauce
45 ml/3 tablespoons Chinese rice
* wine or dry sherry*
105 ml/7 tablespoons corn oil
120 ml/4 fl oz chicken stock
5 ml/1 teaspoon cornflour
30 ml/2 tablespoons water
salt
boiled rice, to serve

Approximately per portion:
2,200 kj/520 kcal
43 g protein
29 g fat
20 g carbohydrate

● Approximate preparation
time: 25 minutes

---

1. Cut the duck breasts into bite-size pieces and put them into a shallow dish.

2. For the marinade, dissolve the honey in the hot water. Stir in the tomato ketchup, Worcestershire sauce, soy sauce and the rice wine or sherry.

3. Pour the marinade over the duck, turning to coat well. Cover and set aside in the refrigerator to marinate for 4–6 hours.

4. Heat the oil in a preheated wok. Drain the duck well and lightly pat dry with kitchen paper. Add the duck to the wok, in batches, and stir-fry until they are brown all over. Keep separating the pieces with chopsticks, so that they do not stick together. Drain the cooked duck thoroughly and keep warm.

5. Pour off the oil from the wok. Add the chicken stock and bring to the boil, stirring to scrape off the meat juices from the wok. Stir in the marinade. Mix together the cornflour and the water to make a smooth paste, then add to the wok. Bring to the boil, stirring, until thickened. Season with salt if necessary. Return the duck to the wok and heat through, stirring constantly. Serve immediately with boiled rice.

Tip

Serve the duck with Chinese-style vegetables. You can buy these frozen and ready-prepared from supermarkets and Chinese stores.

Duck with carrots and almonds

For guests • Exquisite

Serves 4
4 boneless duck breasts (each about
* 150 g/5 oz)*
freshly ground black pepper
15 ml/1 tablespoon ground coriander
salt
600 g/1 lb 5 oz carrots
corn oil, for deep-frying
75 g/3 oz shelled almonds
25 g/1 oz butter
120 ml/4 fl oz chicken stock
5 ml/1 teaspoon clear honey

Approximately per portion:
2,700 kj/640 kcal
40 g protein
47 g fat
13 g carbohydrate

● Approximate preparation
time: 25 minutes

---

1. Make a number of small slashes in the skin of the duck breasts. Season well with pepper and coriander and rub salt into the upper sides. Then wrap the duck in foil and set aside in the refrigerator for about 2 hours.

2. Cut the carrots into matchstick strips about 5 cm/2 inches long.

3. Heat the oil in a preheated wok. Add the duck breasts and deep-fry for about 5 minutes on each side. Drain well and keep warm.

4. Pour off the oil from the wok. Dry-fry the almonds in the wok, stirring constantly. Add the butter. Then add the carrots and cook for about 2 minutes, stirring frequently. Pour over the chicken stock and stir in the honey. Cook for about 5 minutes over a high heat. Season to taste with salt. Carve the duck breast fillets into slices. Transfer the carrots and almonds to 4 individual serving plates, top with the slices of duck and serve immediately.

Above: Honeyed duck
Below: Duck with carrots and almonds

Poussin with ginger

Easy to make • Exquisite

A double poussin is a chicken that is approximately six weeks old and weighs about 1 kg/2¼ lb. Sometimes you may find 2 poussins packaged together and labelled as a 'double poussin'. These are usually chickens between four and six weeks old, weighing 350–500 g/12 oz–1¼ lb. Alternatively, you can prepare this recipe with a small chicken.

Serves 4
5 cm/2 inch piece fresh
   root ginger
2 garlic cloves
2 small green peppers
1 small red pepper
60 ml/4 tablespoons sesame or
   groundnut oil
2 pieces star anise
10 black peppercorns
5 allspice berries
1 double poussin, 2 single poussins
   or 1 small chicken
500 ml/17 fl oz water
90 ml/6 tablespoons dark soy sauce
3 spring onions
30 ml/2 tablespoons Chinese rice
   wine or dry sherry
10 ml/2 teaspoons sugar
fried rice, to serve

Approximately per portion:
2,700 kj/640 kcal
65 g protein
37 g fat
12 g carbohydrate

● Approximate preparation
   time: 1 hour

---

1. Cut off 2 cm/¾ inch of the ginger and chop coarsely. Cut the garlic in half. Core, seed and cut the peppers in half lengthways.

2. Heat 30 ml/2 tablespoons of the oil in a preheated wok. Add the star anise, peppercorns, allspice berries and garlic and stir-fry for 1–2 minutes. Add the poussin or chicken, ginger and 2 green pepper halves. Then add the water and 45 ml/3 tablespoons of the soy sauce. Cover and cook the poussin or chicken, turning it over from time to time, for 30–40 minutes, until tender and cooked through.

3. Meanwhile, finely chop the white part of the spring onions and thinly slice the green parts diagonally. Cut the remaining ginger root into matchstick strips.

4. Cut the remaining peppers into matchstick strips.

5. Remove the poussin or chicken from the wok and discard the cooking liquid. Skin the poussin or chicken and cut the meat off the bones, then into bite-size pieces.

6. Heat the remaining oil in a preheated wok. Add the spring onions, the remaining peppers and the ginger and stir-fry for about 2 minutes, until the onions are translucent. Stir in the remaining soy sauce, the rice wine or sherry and the sugar.

7. Return the poussin or chicken to the wok and heat through, stirring constantly, until well coated with the sauce. Transfer to a warm serving dish and serve immediately with fried rice.

Variation
You can cook duck in the same way. Because of its size it must be cooked cut into 4 pieces. Put the legs in first and add the breast pieces 5 minutes later. The cooking time for the breast is about 30–35 minutes. If you wish, you can skin the breast before cooking. Cut the skin into thin strips and fry it in its own fat until crisp. Sprinkle it with salt and serve it as a garnish to the dish.

Tip

The poussin or chicken acquires a special flavour, if it is lightly smoked in the wok before cooking (see page 5). Use 15 ml/1 tablespoon of any strong tea, such as Lapsang suchong, Keemun or Formosa Oolong. A poussin or chicken that has been smoked beforehand will take 5 minutes less cooking time.

Fresh ginger adds pep to this superb poultry dish.

Pork with oranges

Quick • Easy to make

Serves 4
40 g/1½ oz clarified butter
200 g/7 oz small shallots
600 g/1 lb 5 oz pork fillet
15 ml/1 tablespoon flour
120 ml/4 fl oz dry white wine
120 ml/4 fl oz orange juice
salt
2 oranges
45 ml/3 tablespoons orange
   liqueur (optional)
105 ml/7 tablespoons crème fraîche
10 ml/2 teaspoons pink
   peppercorns
fried noodles, to serve

Approximately per portion:
2,400 kj/570 kcal
30 g protein
38 g fat
19 g carbohydrate

● Approximate preparation
   time: 30 minutes

---

1. Melt the clarified butter in a preheated wok. Add the shallots and stir-fry until browned all over. Meanwhile, cut the pork into thin slices across the grain. Sprinkle over the flour.

2. Remove the shallots from the wok, using a slotted spoon, drain well and keep warm. Add the pork slices to the wok, in batches if necessary, and stir-fry until golden brown all over. Keep the cooked meat warm while you stir-fry the remaining batches.

3. Return the pork and shallots to the wok and add the white wine and orange juice and season to taste with salt. Cover and braise for 5 minutes.

4. Meanwhile, peel the oranges, remove the pith and cut the flesh into segments. Stir the orange segments into the wok and warm through. Stir in the orange liqueur, if using, and the crème fraîche. Season to taste with salt and mix in the pink peppercorns. Transfer to a warm serving dish and serve immediately with fried noodles.

Variation
Instead of oranges you can use a single pink grapefruit. This will give the dish a sweet-and-sour taste, as well as making it look sophisticated and elegant.

Pork with red peppers

Rather time-consuming

Serves 4
2 cm/¾ inch piece fresh
   root ginger
1 garlic clove
600 g/1 lb 5 oz pork shoulder
   or belly
60 ml/4 tablespoons dark
   soy sauce
500 g/1¼ lb small firm potatoes
2 red peppers
4 spring onions
30 ml/2 tablespoons lard or
   sunflower oil
120 ml/4 fl oz chicken stock
45 ml/3 tablespoons dry sherry
5 ml/1 teaspoon sugar
salt

Approximately per portion:
3,400 kj/810 kcal
33 g protein
63 g fat
26 g carbohydrate

● Approximate preparation
   time: 1¼ hours

---

1. Cut the ginger into 4 slices. Put the garlic and ginger slices into a wok. Fit a trivet and fill the wok with hot water to a depth of about 3 cm/1¼ inches.

2. Place the pork on the trivet. Pour over 30 ml/2 tablespoons of the soy sauce, cover and steam for 30 minutes. Remove the wok from the heat and set aside to cool for 20 minutes. Pour away the water.

3. Quarter the potatoes lengthways. Core, seed and cut the red peppers into 2 cm/¾ inch dice. Slice the spring onions into 2 cm/¾ inch long pieces.

4. Cut the pork into 3 cm/1¼ inch dice. Melt the lard or heat the oil in a preheated wok. Add the meat and stir-fry for about 5 minutes, until it is lightly browned. Remove it from the wok and drain well.

5. Add the potatoes, peppers and spring onions to the wok and stir-fry for about 5 minutes. Add the chicken stock, sherry, the remaining soy sauce and the sugar. Season to taste with salt. Return the pork to the wok and braise for a further 15 minutes. Serve hot.

Above: Pork with oranges
Below: Pork with red peppers

Spareribs

Good value

Serves 4
1 kg/2¼ lb pork spareribs
15 ml/1 tablespoon vegetable
*   stock granules*
about 1 litre/1¾ pints boiling water
105 ml/7 tablespoons cornflour
250 ml/8 fl oz groundnut or soy oil
30 ml/2 tablespoons tomato juice
30 ml/2 tablespoons tomato
*   ketchup*
30 ml/2 tablespoons clear honey
30 ml/2 tablespoons rice or
*   apple vinegar*
45 ml/3 tablespoons soy sauce

Approximately per portion:
4,800 kj/1,100 kcal
38 g protein
95 g fat
34 g carbohydrate

● Approximate preparation
   time: 35 minutes

I. Chop the meat into individual ribs with a cleaver. Put them into a wok with the stock granules and pour in enough boiling water just to cover the ribs. Bring back to the boil and cook, uncovered, for about 10 minutes.

2. Remove the ribs from the wok, drain and dry well on kitchen paper. Roll them in the cornflour and press it in well.

3. Dry the wok and preheat. Heat the oil in it. Add the ribs and fry, turning constantly, for 5–6 minutes, until they are crispy. Remove them with a slotted spoon or wok scoop and drain well on kitchen paper.

4. Pour off nearly all the oil. Add the tomato juice, tomato ketchup, honey, vinegar and soy sauce to the wok and cook, stirring constantly, for 3 minutes. Return the spareribs to the wok and braise, turning and stirring to coat thoroughly, for 10 minutes, until they are tender. Serve immediately.

Pork with peanuts

Quick • Good value

Serves 4
1 red pepper
2 medium onions
2 garlic cloves
75 g/3 oz unsalted shelled peanuts
50 g/2 oz cellophane noodles
90 ml/6 tablespoons groundnut or
*   sesame oil*
500 g/1¼ lb minced pork
15 ml/1 tablespoon cornflour
120 ml/4 fl oz chicken stock
30 ml/2 tablespoons oyster sauce
30 ml/2 tablespoons soy sauce
30 ml/2 tablespoons Chinese rice
*   wine or dry sherry*
sugar
boiled rice, to serve

Approximately per portion:
2,600 kj/620 kcal
40 g protein
45 g fat
15 g carbohydrate

● Approximate preparation
   time: 35 minutes

I. Core, seed and finely dice the red pepper. Finely dice the onions and finely chop the garlic.

2. Heat a wok and add the peanuts. Dry-fry, stirring constantly, for about 3 minutes. Remove the peanuts from the wok and set aside for the garnish.

3. Cut the noodles into 5 cm/ 2 inch long pieces with kitchen scissors. Heat the oil in a preheated wok. Add the noodles and fry for about 30 seconds. Remove from the wok and drain on kitchen paper.

4. Add the pepper, onions and garlic to the wok and stir-fry, until the onions are transparent. Add the pork and stir-fry it until it has broken up and just changed colour. Sprinkle over the cornflour and stir.

5. Stir in the chicken stock, oyster sauce, soy sauce, Chinese rice wine or sherry and a pinch of sugar. Lower the heat and simmer, stirring constantly, for about 5 minutes. Transfer to a deep serving dish, garnish with the peanuts and noodles and serve immediately with boiled rice.

Tip

Soak dried cellophane noodles in water for about 15 minutes before cutting and frying them.

Above: Spareribs
Below: Pork with peanuts

Meatballs with tomatoes

Family favourite

Serves 4
1 kg/2¼ lb small ripe tomatoes
40 g/1½ oz butter
2 garlic cloves
salt
freshly ground white pepper
1 bunch fresh parsley
3 spring onions
300 g/11 oz minced pork
300 g/11 oz minced beef
1 large egg
pinch of ground ginger
pinch of ground coriander
90 ml/6 tablespoons fresh
   white breadcrumbs
120 ml/4 fl oz groundnut or soy oil
boiled rice, to serve

Approximately per portion:
2,800 kj/670 kcal
41 g protein
44 g fat
29 g carbohydrate

● Approximate preparation
   time: 35 minutes

1. Blanch the tomatoes in boiling water for 1–2 minutes. Drain, skin, seed and quarter the flesh. Melt the butter in a preheated wok. Add the tomatoes. Crush the garlic over them.

2. Season the tomatoes to taste with salt and pepper and cook over a very low heat until they become runny. Meanwhile, finely chop the parsley. Thinly slice the spring onions.

3. Mix together the pork, beef, parsley, spring onions and the egg. Season to taste with salt, pepper, ginger and coriander. With damp hands, form the mixture into balls about the size of a golf ball. Put the breadcrumbs on a plate and roll the meatballs in them to coat.

4. Remove the tomatoes from the wok. Clean and re-heat the wok. Heat the oil in the wok. Add the meatballs and fry, turning them constantly, until they are crispy brown all over. Remove and drain. Return the tomatoes to the wok and heat through. Transfer the tomatoes to a serving dish, top with the meat meatballs and serve immediately with boiled rice.

Tip

To serve, press boiled rice into an oiled ring mould and turn it out on to a serving plate. Put the tomatoes in the middle and arrange the meatballs on top.

Beef rolls with carrots and beans

Exotic

Serves 4
200 g/7 oz green beans
salt
200 g/7 oz young carrots
4 spring onions
4 slices lean beef
  (each about 200 g/7 oz)
10 ml/2 teaspoons horseradish sauce
5 ml/1 teaspoon cornflour
120 ml/4 fl oz groundnut or soy oil
5 ml/1 teaspoon flour
200 ml/7 fl oz beef extract
105 ml/7 tablespoons medium
  dry sherry
75 ml/5 tablespoons soy sauce
dash of Worcestershire sauce
5 ml/1 teaspoon pink peppercorns,
  to garnish
flat noodles, to serve

Approximately per portion:
2,400 kj/570 kcal
58 g protein
31 g fat
15 g carbohydrate

● Approximate preparation
  time: 1 hour

Tip

Japanese udon noodles go particularly well with these beef rolls. You can buy them in Chinese and Japanese supermarkets. Otherwise, you can use narrow flat noodles, tossed in a little butter.

1. Trim and string the beans, if necessary. Blanch in lightly salted boiling water for about 5 minutes. Drain, refresh in cold water, drain again and set aside. Cut the carrots into thin strips and blanch in lightly salted boiling water for about 3 minutes. Drain, refresh in cold water, drain again and set aside. Cut the spring onions crossways in half.

2. Stretch the beef slices out as flat and as thin as possible and cut in half lengthways. Spread with the horseradish sauce and arrange the vegetables equally across the slices. Roll them up, secure with cocktail sticks and sprinkle with cornflour.

3. Heat the oil in a preheated wok. Add the beef rolls, a few at a time, and fry, turning frequently, for about 10 minutes. Remove and drain well. Pour off all but 15 ml/ 1 tablespoon of the oil and return the wok to the heat. Stir in the flour. Add the beef extract, sherry and soy sauce and stir thoroughly.

4. Return the beef rolls to the wok, cover and braise for 30–35 minutes. Remove the lid, increase the heat to high and cook, turning the beef rolls constantly, for a further 5 minutes to reduce the liquid. Season to taste with Worcestershire sauce. Transfer the rolls to a serving dish, sprinkle over the pink peppercorns and serve with flat noodles.

Hot-and-sour beef

For beginners

This savoury stir-fried meat dish comes from the province of Hunan in the north part of central China. It is known as 'the land of fish and rice', but it is also famous for its piquant sweet-and-sour and hot-and-sour sauces.

Serves 4
600 g/1 lb 5 oz rump steak
1 egg white
30 ml/2 tablespoons cornflour
30 ml/2 tablespoons sesame oil
freshly ground black pepper
4 cm/1½ inch piece fresh
  root ginger
2–3 garlic cloves
2 medium carrots
250 g/9 oz can bamboo
  shoots, drained
2 small leeks
1 red or green pepper
200 ml/7 fl oz corn oil
60 ml/4 tablespoons soy sauce
60 ml/4 tablespoons chicken stock
30 ml/2 tablespoons Chinese rice
  wine or dry sherry
30 ml/2 tablespoons rice or
  apple vinegar

Approximately per portion:
3,100 kj/740 kcal
42 g protein
53 g fat
22 g carbohydrate

- Freezing time: about 30 minutes

- Approximate preparation time: 45 minutes

---

1. Wrap the meat in a freezer bag, seal and put it into the freezer for about 30 minutes, until it is just beginning to freeze. This makes it easier to slice extremely thinly. Using an electric carving knife or a very sharp knife, cut the steak into very thin slices.

2. Beat the egg white until it forms soft peaks. Stir in 7.5 ml/ 1½ teaspoons of the cornflour and a few drops of sesame oil. Season the steak with pepper, cover it with the egg white mixture and set aside for about 15 minutes.

3. Meanwhile, finely chop the ginger and garlic.

4. Thinly slice the carrots. Thinly slice the bamboo shoots, then cut into strips about 1 cm/½ inch wide and 3 cm/1¼ inches long. Thinly slice the white part of the leeks diagonally.

5. Core and seed the red or green pepper and cut the flesh into very thin strips.

6. Reserve 45 ml/3 tablespoons of the corn oil. Heat the remaining oil in a preheated wok. Add the meat and stir-fry until browned on all sides. With a slotted spoon, remove the meat from the wok and keep warm.

7. Pour off the oil, wipe the wok with kitchen paper and re-heat. Heat the remaining corn oil in the wok. Add the ginger, garlic, carrots and bamboo shoots and stir-fry for about 1 minute. Add the pepper, soy sauce and chicken stock and cook, stirring constantly, for a few more seconds.

8. Mix the remaining cornflour with the Chinese rice wine or sherry to make a smooth paste. Return the meat to the wok, add the leeks and cook, stirring constantly, for a further 15 seconds. Stir in the cornflour paste and vinegar and cook, stirring, until slightly thickened. Serve immediately, sprinkled with the remaining sesame oil.

Tip

Chinese rice wine is available from Chinese and Asian supermarkets. It has a distinctive, rich flavour, rather like sherry, and is quite different from Japanese saki. The best Chinese rice wine is thought to be Shaohsing.

Wafer-thin Hot-and-sour beef and fresh vegetables makes a delicious wok dish, ideal for when you have guests.

Beef with celery

Exquisite • Easy to make

Serves 4–6
750 g/1 lb 10 oz boneless leg
    of beef
1–2 garlic cloves
1 head of celery
50 g/2 oz clarified butter
90 g/3½ oz shelled walnuts
12 small shallots
salt
freshly ground white pepper
5 ml/1 teaspoon flour
120 ml/4 fl oz strong red wine
30 ml/2 tablespoons crème fraîche
dash of Worcestershire sauce
flat noodles, to serve

For 6 people, approximately per portion:
1,800 kj/430 kcal
30 g protein
30 g fat
7 g carbohydrate

● Approximate preparation
  time: 45 minutes

---

1. Cut the beef into thin strips.

2. Finely chop the garlic. Cut the celery into chunks about 1 cm/ ½ inch thick.

3. Melt half the clarified butter in a preheated wok and add the walnuts, a few at a time, and stir-fry for a few seconds. Remove with a slotted spoon and set aside.

4. Melt the remaining clarified butter in the wok. Add the shallots and garlic and stir-fry briefly until they become translucent. Add the meat, in batches, and stir-fry until it is brown all over. Season to taste with salt and pepper and sprinkle over the flour.

5. Pour in the red wine and add the celery. Bring to the boil and cook, stirring constantly, over a high heat for about 5 minutes.

6. Add the crème fraîche, season with Worcestershire sauce and scatter over the walnuts. Transfer to a warm serving dish and serve immediately with flat noodles.

Beef with pineapple

For guests

Serves 4
600 g/1 lb 5 oz sliced lean beef
250 g/9 oz can pineapple chunks
    in juice
40 g/1½ oz clarified butter
salt
freshly ground white pepper
15 ml/1 tablespoon flour
200 ml/7 fl oz beef extract
105 ml/7 tablespoons light red wine
50 g/2 oz chopped almonds,
    to garnish
ribbon noodles, to serve

Approximately per portion:
2,300 kj/550 kcal
47 g protein
32 g fat
9 g carbohydrate

● Approximate preparation
  time: 35 minutes

---

1. Slice the beef diagonally across the grain into strips about 1 cm/ ½ inch wide.

2. Drain the pineapple chunks and reserve the juice. Melt the clarified butter in a preheated wok. Add the pineapple chunks and stir-fry until they are golden brown. Remove with a slotted spoon and set aside.

3. Add the beef and stir-fry until it is browned all over. Season to taste with salt and pepper and sprinkle over the flour. Stir in the beef extract, red wine and 30–45 ml/2–3 tablespoons of the reserved pineapple juice. Cover and braise for about 10 minutes. Mix in the pineapple chunks and heat through. Transfer to a serving dish, sprinkle over the almonds and serve with ribbon noodles.

Tip

If you have time, you can use fresh pineapple instead of canned. The enzyme bromelin, which is only found in fresh pineapple, makes the meat very tender. If you use canned fruit, you can add 20 ml/4 teaspoons brandy to the braising liquid, which will also help to make the meat tender.

Above: Beef with celery
Below: Beef with pineapple

Beef with mushrooms and onions

For beginners

Chinese black mushrooms of varying quality can be found in Asian shops. The basic rule is: the bigger, the better. Do not buy broken mushrooms.

Serves 4
20 g/¾ oz dried Chinese black mushrooms
500 g/1¼ lb slices lean beef
10 ml/2 teaspoons cornflour
500 g/1¼ lb onions
1 large green pepper
1 large red pepper
60 ml/4 tablespoons groundnut or soy oil
120 ml/4 fl oz chicken stock
30–45 ml/2–3 tablespoons oyster sauce
salt
cayenne pepper
ground coriander
boiled rice, to serve

Approximately per portion:
1,900 kj/450 kcal
38 g protein
25 g fat
18 g carbohydrate

● Approximate preparation time: 25 minutes

1. Put the mushrooms in a bowl and add just enough lukewarm water to cover. Set aside to soak for 20–30 minutes. Drain and squeeze out excess moisture. Cut off and discard the hard stalks and halve or quarter the caps, according to size.

2. Cut the meat across the grain into very thin strips. Sprinkle over the cornflour and rub it in well with your fingertips.

3. Cut the onions in half, then thinly slice.

4. Core and seed the green and red peppers and cut the flesh into small diamond-shapes.

5. Heat the oil in a preheated wok. Add the onions and stir-fry until they are golden brown. Remove with a slotted spoon.

6. Add the beef to the wok and stir-fry until it is brown all over. Add the peppers and mushrooms and stir-fry for 1 minute. Stir in the chicken stock and oyster sauce and bring to the boil.

7. Return the onions to the wok and heat through. Season to taste with salt, cayenne pepper and ground coriander. Serve immediately with boiled rice.

Tip

Do not throw away the water in which the mushrooms were soaked. It is full of flavour. Strain it through a coffee filter paper, then boil over a high heat until reduced by at least one third. Set aside to cool, then freeze in an ice-cube tray wrapped in a freezer bag. Then you can use individual mushroom stock cubes as required. This stock can be used, not only with dishes cooked in the wok, but also to add flavour to other braised dishes.

Variation
Instead of beef, you can use a lean cut of lamb, such as loin.

Beef with mushrooms and onions is stir-fried in the wok and seasoned with oyster sauce and spices to add piquancy.

Veal with cherry sauce

Quick

Serves 4
4 veal escalopes
*   (each about 185 g/6½ oz)*
30 ml/2 tablespoons flour
salt
freshly ground white pepper
25 g/1 oz clarified butter
250 g/9 oz stoned Morello cherries
105 ml/7 tablespoons unsweetened
*   cherry juice*
105 ml/7 tablespoons light red wine
50 ml/2 fl oz crème fraîche
2.5 ml/½ teaspoon ground
*   cardamom*
ground ginger

Approximately per portion:
1,600 kj/380 kcal
39 g protein
15 g fat
17 g carbohydrate

● Approximate preparation
   time: 20 minutes

---

1. Place the veal escalopes between two layers of clear film and beat them as thin as possible with the flat side of a meat hammer or with a rolling pin. Cut them in half lengthways and then cut each half into 4 pieces.

2. Mix the flour with salt and pepper and spread it out on a plate. Toss the meat in it and press to ensure that it is coated thoroughly. Heat the clarified butter in a preheated wok. Add the meat and fry, turning and stirring frequently, until browned all over. Remove from the wok with a slotted spoon and keep warm.

3. Put the cherries in the wok, together with the cherry juice and red wine and bring to the boil. Return the veal to the wok, lower the heat and simmer for about 5 minutes.

4. Stir in the crème fraîche and season to taste with salt, pepper, cardamom and ginger. Transfer to a serving dish and serve immediately.

Veal with apples and cider

For guests

Serves 4–6
800 g/1¾ lb loin of veal
3 cooking apples
15 ml/1 tablespoon lemon juice
3 spring onions
12 plums, stoned
30 ml/2 tablespoons flour
salt
freshly ground white pepper
50 g/2 oz clarified butter
200 ml/7 fl oz cider or apple juice
20 ml/4 teaspoons Calvados
boiled mixed long grain and wild
*   rice, to serve*

**For 6 persons
approximately per portion:**
1,300 kj/310 kcal
29 g protein,
11 g fat
20 g carbohydrate

● Approximate preparation
   time: 35 minutes

---

1. Cut the meat in half lengthways and then cut it into thin strips.

2. Peel, quarter and core the apples and cut lengthways into thin strips. Mix them with the lemon juice to prevent discolouration.

3. Thinly slice the spring onions diagonally into rings. Quarter the plums lengthways.

4. Season the flour with salt and pepper and put it on a plate. Toss the meat in it. Melt the clarified butter in a preheated wok. Add the meat and stir-fry until browned all over. Remove with a slotted spoon and keep warm.

5. Add the apples and spring onions to the wok and stir-fry until the onions are translucent. Stir in the cider or apple juice, then add the plums. Return the veal to the wok and bring to the boil. Boil over a high heat for 2–3 minutes. Stir in the Calvados and season to taste with salt and pepper. Serve with a mixture of boiled long grain and wild rice.

Above: Veal with cherry sauce
Below: Veal with apples and cider

Plaice fillets with ham

Exquisite

Serves 4
2 cm/3/4 inch piece fresh
    root ginger
2 spring onions or shallots
115 g/4 oz button mushrooms
8 plaice fillets
    (each about 75 g/3 oz)
10 ml/2 teaspoons raspberry or
    sherry vinegar
salt
freshly ground white pepper
4 thin slices Parma ham
200 ml/7 fl oz fish stock
200 ml/7 fl oz dry white wine
30 ml/2 tablespoons crème fraîche
grilled tomatoes and boiled rice and
    peas or creamed potatoes,
    to serve

Approximately per portion:
1,300 kj/310 kcal
31 g protein
14 g fat
5 g carbohydrate

● Approximate preparation
    time: 25 minutes

1. Thinly slice the root ginger.
Thinly slice the spring onions or
shallots and push out into rings.
Slice the mushrooms.

2. Brush the plaice fillets with the
vinegar. Season lightly with salt and
pepper. Place 1 slice of Parma ham
on each of 4 of the plaice fillets
and divide the mushrooms
between them. Put the remaining
fish fillets on top.

3. Put the ginger and spring onions
or shallots into the wok and fit the
trivet. Mix together the fish stock
and wine and pour in just enough
to reach 1 cm/1/2 inch below the
trivet. Reserve the remainder.
Bring the liquid to the boil.

4. Arrange the fish fillets on the
trivet, cover and steam for about
10 minutes. Remove the fish from
the wok, transfer to a serving dish
and keep warm.

5. Strain the cooking liquid and
return it to the wok. Add the
reserved stock mixture. Boil over a
high heat until reduced by about
one third. Stir in the crème fraîche
and season to taste with salt and
pepper. Serve the fish with grilled
tomatoes and boiled rice and peas
or creamed potatoes. Hand the
sauce separately.

Fish balls with ginger

Rather time-consuming

Serves 4
500 g/1 1/4 lb cod or haddock fillets
4 shallots
2 cm/3/4 inch piece fresh root ginger
1/2 bunch fresh coriander or flat
    leaf parsley
30–45 ml/2–3 tablespoons iced
    water
30 ml/2 tablespoons cornflour
1 egg
1 egg yolk
salt
freshly ground white pepper
lemon juice
groundnut or soy oil, for deep-frying

Approximately per portion:
920 kj/220 kcal
26 g protein
7 g fat
13 g carbohydrate

● Approximate preparation
    time: 1 hour 10 minutes

1. Remove any remaining bones
from the fish fillets. Finely chop the
shallots. Roughly chop the ginger.
Pull the leaves off the coriander or
parsley stalks. Put the fish, shallots,
ginger and coriander or parsley
into a food processor and work to
make a fine mixture.

2. Knead the mixture into a dough
with the water, 15 ml/1 tablespoon
of the cornflour, the egg and egg
yolk. Season to taste with salt,
pepper and lemon juice. Use damp
hands to form the mixture into
balls about the size of a tennis ball.

3. Dust the balls with the
remaining cornflour and chill in the
refrigerator for about 30 minutes.

4. Heat the oil in the wok until it is
smoking. Add the balls, in batches,
and fry until they are browned all
over. Drain on kitchen paper and
serve hot.

Above: Plaice fillets with ham
Below: Fish balls with ginger

Smoked trout with herb sauce

Easy to make

Serves 2
2 bunches fresh dill
1 bunch fresh parsley
2 lovage sprigs
1 carrot
1 small onion
105 ml/7 tablespoons dry
   white wine
105 ml/7 tablespoons fish stock
2 smoked trout
   (each about 300 g/10½ oz)
105 ml/7 tablespoons double cream
25 g/1 oz cold butter, cut into pieces
salt
freshly ground white pepper
dill sprigs, to garnish
steamed broccoli and baked
   potatoes, to serve

Approximately per portion:
2,800 kj/670 kcal
64 g protein
37 g fat
13 g carbohydrate

● Approximate preparation
   time: 40 minutes

---

1. Pull the dill, parsley and lovage leaves of the stalks and chop finely. Roughly chop the carrot and onion.

2. Mix together the white wine and fish stock. Fill the wok to a depth of about 2 cm/¾ inch with the mixture. Reserve the remainder. Reserve 30 ml/ 2 tablespoons of the herbs and add the remainder to the wok, together with the carrot and onion. Fit the trivet and lay the trout on it. Cover and steam for 10–12 minutes. Remove the trout from the wok and keep warm.

3. Strain the liquid into a saucepan. Stir in the remaining wine and fish stock mixture and the cream. Bring to the boil over a high heat and allow to reduce by about one third. Stir the butter into the sauce, one piece at a time, beating until each piece is fully incorporated before adding the next.

4. Season the sauce to taste with salt and white pepper and add the reserved mixed herbs. Keep the sauce warm. Fillet and skin the trout and divide between individual serving plates. Spoon the sauce on to the plates beside the trout fillets. Garnish with fresh dill sprigs and serve with baked potatoes and steamed broccoli.

Variation
Other smoked fish, such as monkfish, halibut or swordfish, can be substituted for the trout in this recipe. By using the wok for smoking the fish yourself, you can easily and economically obtain some more unusual varieties.
   You can also prepare smoked duck breasts in the same way, substituting sage for the lovage and chicken stock for the fish stock.

Tip

Smoked trout will keep for 2–3 days if wrapped loosely in greaseproof paper and stored in the refrigerator. Vacuum-packed smoked trout will keep for several days longer.

Smoked trout with a delicate and aromatic herb sauce is simply delicious.

Eel with lemon and herb butter

Easy to make

Once very popular, freshwater eel has rather gone out of fashion, but it is still available. The flesh is firm, white, sweet and very rich. The fishmonger will prepare it for you.

Serves 4
800 g/1¾ lb cleaned, skinned eel
salt
60 ml/4 tablespoons wine vinegar
1 bunch mixed fresh herbs
1 lemon
75 ml/5 tablespoons flour
freshly ground white pepper
50 g/2 oz clarified butter
75 g/3 oz butter
new potatoes and mixed salad,
  to serve

Approximately per portion:
3,900 kj/930 kcal
34 g protein
78 g fat
22 g carbohydrate

● Approximate preparation
  time: 35 minutes

---

1. Rub the eel with salt, rinse and pat dry. Cut it into pieces about 5–6 cm/2–2½ inch long and put them into a bowl. Pour over the wine vinegar and set aside for about 10 minutes.

2. Finely chop the mixed herbs. Grate the lemon rind and squeeze out the juice.

3. Put the flour on a shallow plate and season with a little salt and plenty of pepper. Dry the eel pieces well and roll them in the flour to coat thoroughly.

4. Melt the clarified butter in a preheated wok. Add the eel pieces, a few at a time, and stir fry for 6–8 minutes, until they are golden brown all over. Drain on kitchen paper.

5. Drain and wipe the wok. Melt the butter in the wok. Add the herbs, lemon rind and juice and return the eel pieces to the wok to heat through. Transfer the eel to a serving dish and pour over the lemon and herb butter. Serve immediately with new potatoes and a mixed salad.

Sardines with capers and Parmesan cheese

For guests

Serves 4
12 fresh sardines, cleaned
60 ml/4 tablespoons lemon juice
4 slices day-old white bread
1 bunch flat leaf parsley
30 ml/2 tablespoons olive oil
1 egg yolk
15 ml/1 tablespoon capers
60 ml/4 tablespoons freshly grated
  Parmesan cheese
salt
freshly ground white pepper
flour for dusting
50 g/2 oz clarified butter
2 lemons
fresh flat leaf parsley sprigs,
  to garnish

Approximately per portion:
2,700 kj/640 kcal
49 g protein
39 g fat
29 g carbohydrate

● Approximate preparation
  time: 30 minutes

---

1. Slit the sardines open along the undersides. Rinse them well under cold running water and sprinkle with lemon juice.

2. Cut the crusts from the white bread. Put the bread, parsley, oil, egg yolk, capers and cheese in a food processor and work to a smooth paste. Season the mixture to taste with salt and pepper.

3. Lay the sardines out flat on a work surface and divide the cheese mixture between them, spreading it out evenly. Roll up the fish and secure with cocktail sticks. Dust them with flour.

4. Melt the clarified butter in a preheated wok. Add the fish rolls, in batches if necessary, and stir-fry for 2–3 minutes. Remove the fish rolls from the wok and keep warm.

5. Thinly slice the lemons. Place the lemon slices on a serving plate, arrange the sardine rolls on top, garnish with the flat leaf parsley and serve immediately.

Above: Eel with lemon and herb butter
Below: Sardines with capers and Parmesan cheese

Cod with ginger sauce

Superb

Serves 4
600 g/1 lb 5 oz cod fillets
75 ml/5 tablespoons dry white wine
salt
2 spring onions
4 cm/1½ inch piece fresh
    root ginger
1 garlic clove
200 ml/7 fl oz groundnut or soy oil
2 eggs
60 ml/4 tablespoons flour
15 ml/1 tablespoon sesame seeds
200 ml/7 fl oz chicken stock
30 ml/2 tablespoons soy sauce
10 ml/2 teaspoons cornflour
45 ml/3 tablespoons water
sugar
30 ml/2 tablespoons green
    peppercorns

Approximately per portion:
2,635 kj/630 kcal
46 g protein
36 g fat
26 g carbohydrate

● Approximate preparation
  time: 30 minutes

1. Cut the fish into 5 cm/2 inch chunks. Sprinkle over a little of the wine and season with salt.

2. Thinly slice the spring onions diagonally. Finely chop the ginger and garlic.

3. Reserve 30 ml/2 tablespoons of the oil and heat the remainder in a preheated wok until it is smoking.

Lightly beat the eggs together. Dip the fish chunks into the beaten egg, then dust them with flour. Add them to the wok and fry until crispy brown all over. Drain on kitchen paper.

4. Pour off the oil and clean the wok. Heat the remaining oil in the wok. Add the sesame seeds, then add the onions, ginger and garlic and stir-fry for about 10 seconds.

5. Pour in the remaining wine, the chicken stock and soy sauce. Mix together the cornflour and water to make a smooth paste, add it to the sauce and cook, stirring constantly, until thickened. Season with salt, a pinch of sugar and the peppercorns. Return the fish chunks to the wok to heat through, turning them carefully to coat thoroughly. Serve immediately.

Prawns with ham

Rather expensive

Serves 4
1 thick slice raw ham
    (about 115 g/4 oz)
2 small spring onions
500 g/1¼ lb raw, peeled
    tiger prawns
45 ml/3 tablespoons cornflour
200 ml/7 fl oz groundnut or soy oil
250 g/9 oz frozen peas, thawed
200 ml/7 fl oz chicken stock
30–45 ml/2–3 tablespoons light
    soy sauce
30–45 ml/2–3 tablespoons Chinese
    rice wine or dry sherry
45 ml/3 tablespoons water
salt
freshly ground black pepper

Approximately per portion:
2,300 kj/550 kcal
35 g protein
39 g fat
14 g carbohydrate

● Approximate preparation
  time: 25 minutes

1. Cut the ham into 1 cm/½ inch cubes. Thinly slice the spring onions diagonally.

2. Devein the prawns. Lightly sprinkle over a little cornflour.

3. Reserve 30 ml/2 tablespoons of the oil and heat the remainder in a preheated wok. Add the prawns, in batches if necessary, and stir-fry for about 10 seconds, until they change colour. Remove with a slotted spoon and drain well on kitchen paper.

4. Pour off the oil and wipe out the wok. Return the wok to the heat and heat the remaining oil. Add the peas, ham and spring onions and stir-fry for about 10 seconds. Pour in the chicken stock, soy sauce and the rice wine or sherry. Mix the remaining cornflour with the water to form a smooth paste. Stir it into the wok and cook, stirring constantly, until the sauce has thickened.

5. Return the prawns to the wok to heat through and season to taste with salt and pepper. Serve immediately.

Above: Cod with ginger sauce
Below: Prawns with ham

Prawns with peppers

For guests • Rather expensive

This is a slightly Westernized version of a dish from the Chinese province of Hunan. This province has the most fertile soil in China and arguably the best cuisine in the whole country.

Serves 4
500 g/1¼ lb raw, peeled
   tiger prawns
1 egg white
15 ml/1 tablespoon cornflour
1 red pepper
1 green pepper
1 yellow pepper
1 small fresh green chilli
1 garlic clove
3 cm/1¼ inch piece fresh
   root ginger
1 small thin leek
200 ml/7 fl oz groundnut or soy oil
90 ml/6 tablespoons chicken stock
30–45 ml/2–3 tablespoons dark
   soy sauce
15 ml/1 tablespoon rice or
   apple vinegar
salt
10 ml/2 teaspoons sesame oil

Approximately per portion:
2,000 kj/480 kcal
34 g protein
32 g fat
14 g carbohydrate

● Approximate preparation
   time: 30 minutes

---

1. Devein the prawns. Lightly beat the egg white with a fork and mix in half the cornflour. Add the prawns and mix well together.

2. Core and seed the red, green and yellow peppers and cut the flesh into diamond shapes about 2 cm/¾ inch long.

3. Seed and finely chop the green chilli. Finely chop or crush the garlic and finely chop the ginger. Thinly slice the white part of the leek diagonally. Cut the tender green parts of the leek into diamond shapes.

4. Heat the oil in a preheated wok until it is smoking. Add the prawns, in batches if necessary, and stir-fry for about 10 seconds, until they change colour. Drain on kitchen paper. Pour off all but about 45 ml/ 3 tablespoons of the oil from the wok and return it to the heat.

5. Add the peppers, chilli, garlic, ginger and leek to the wok and stir-fry for about 10 seconds. Then add the chicken stock and cook, stirring constantly, for 30 seconds.

6. Mix the remaining cornflour with the soy sauce to make a smooth paste. Stir the cornflour mixture into the wok and bring back to the boil. Stir in the vinegar and season to taste with salt. Return the prawns to the wok and heat through, stirring continually. Transfer to a warm serving dish, sprinkle over the sesame oil and serve immediately.

Tip

To be more typically Chinese, you could season the dish with only a little soy sauce, but add a hot bean paste as well. This paste is used in Hunan at nearly every meal. It is made of soy bean paste mixed with chopped chillies fried in oil. You can obtain it from Chinese and Asian shops. Other soy bean pastes are also available. The 'standard' bean paste is also known as brown bean sauce. It is very salty and is virtually a thicker version of soy sauce. Sweet bean paste, also called red bean paste, is often used for dips or for brushing pancakes. It can be used as a base for sweet sauces, which usually go well with seafood.

You can also use a wok to create delicious stir-fried dishes with a range of seafood – these Prawns with peppers taste wonderful!

Red-cooked scampi

Exquisite

This dish from Shanghai can also be prepared using tiger prawns.

Serves 4
16–20 large raw scampi
75 ml/5 tablespoons tomato
*   ketchup*
15 ml/1 tablespoon brown sugar or
*   clear honey*
45–60 ml/3–4 tablespoons dark
*   soy sauce*
60 ml/4 tablespoons Chinese rice
*   wine or dry sherry*
15 ml/1 tablespoon rice or
*   apple vinegar*
salt
2 cm/¾ inch piece fresh root ginger
2 spring onions
90 ml/6 tablespoons groundnut or
*   soy oil*
French bread, to serve

Approximately per portion:
1,900 kj/450 kcal
25 g protein
32 g fat
16 g carbohydrate

● Approximate preparation
   time: 30 minutes

Tip

Follow the European custom and serve the scampi with fresh French bread to soak up the delicious sauce.

1. Cut through the scampi shells on the underside with sharp kitchen scissors.

2. Mix together the tomato ketchup, sugar or honey, soy sauce, rice wine or sherry and the vinegar in a bowl. Season the sauce with salt, if necessary.

3. Slice the ginger, then cut into very thin strips. Finely chop the spring onions. Heat the oil in a preheated wok until it is smoking. Add the scampi, in batches if necessary, and stir-fry until they are red. Remove from the wok and keep warm. Pour off all but 30 ml/2 tablespoons of the oil from the wok and return it to the heat.

4. Add the ginger and onions to the wok and stir-fry for about 10 seconds. Add the sauce and bring to the boil. Return the scampi to the wok and cook in the sauce until heated through and well coated. Arrange the scampi on 4 individual serving plates with all the heads pointing in the same direction and serve immediately with French bread.

Chinese prawn omelette

Easy to make

Serves 4
250 g/9 oz peeled, cooked prawns
30 ml/2 tablespoons soy sauce
30 ml/2 tablespoons Chinese rice
*   wine or dry sherry*
2 spring onions
6 eggs
6 drops sesame oil
salt
freshly ground white pepper
90 ml/6 tablespoons groundnut oil
25 g/1 oz butter

Approximately per portion:
2,200 kj/520 kcal
24 g protein
46 g fat
3 g carbohydrate

● Approximate preparation
  time: 15 minutes

Tip

You can use any variety of
prawns for this omelette, such
as Mediterranean or deep-sea.
You could also make it with
thawed frozen crabmeat.

1. Devein the prawns, rinse and
pat dry. Mix together the soy sauce
and the rice wine or sherry, add
the prawns and set aside for about
5 minutes.

2. Meanwhile, finely chop the
white part of the spring onions.
Thinly slice the green part
diagonally. Keep them separate.
Beat the eggs with the sesame oil.
Season to taste with salt and
white pepper.

3. Heat the groundnut oil in a
preheated wok. Drain the prawns
and pat dry. Add to the wok and
stir-fry for about 2 minutes.
Remove the prawns from the wok
and drain on kitchen paper. Pour
off the hot oil and return the wok
to the heat.

4. Melt the butter in the wok. Add
the white part of the spring onions
and stir fry for about 1 minute,
until translucent. Pour in the
beaten egg mixture and cook,
stirring constantly. As soon as it
begins to set, mix in the prawns.
Cook until the mixture is just set,
but still creamy. Serve immediately,
garnished with the green part of
the spring onions.

Sesame-coated tofu with mushrooms

Quick

Serves 4
500 g/1¼ lb tofu
½ bunch fresh parsley
½ bunch chives
500 g/1¼ lb chestnut mushrooms
10 ml/2 teaspoons herb vinegar
1 egg
salt
cayenne pepper
15 ml/1 tablespoon cornflour
120 ml/4 fl oz groundnut or soy oil
60 ml/4 tablespoons sesame seeds
25 g/1 oz butter

Approximately per portion:
2,000 kj/480 kcal
20 g protein
38 g fat
12 g carbohydrate

● Approximate preparation
time: 35 minutes

---

1. Drain the tofu. Wrap each block separately in a cloth and carefully press it out, without breaking the tofu. Then cut each block in half across. Pat dry.

2. Finely chop the parsley and snip the chives. Slice the mushrooms and mix them with the vinegar.

3. Beat the egg. Season to taste with salt and cayenne pepper. Sprinkle the tofu cubes with the cornflour. Heat the oil in a preheated wok.

4. Dip the tofu cubes first in egg, then in sesame seeds to coat. Add the tofu to the wok and fry until crispy brown on all sides. Drain on kitchen paper and keep warm.

5. Pour the oil out of the wok and return it to the heat. Melt the butter, then add the chestnut mushrooms and stir-fry for 2 minutes. Stir in the parsley and chives. Arrange the mushrooms on a serving dish, top with tofu cubes and serve immediately.

Tofu with peppers

Good value

Serves 4
500 g/1¼ lb tofu
500 g/1¼ lb mixed peppers
1 fresh green chilli
2 garlic cloves
2 medium onions
50 g/2 oz pine nuts
90 ml/6 tablespoons groundnut or
    soy oil
60 ml/4 tablespoons soy sauce
60 ml/4 tablespoons Chinese rice
    wine or dry sherry
120 ml/4 fl oz vegetable stock
5 ml/1 teaspoon cornflour
30 ml/2 tablespoons water
boiled rice, to serve

Approximately per portion:
2,300 kj/550 kcal
22 g protein
41 g fat
21 g carbohydrate

● Approximate preparation
time: 45 minutes

---

1. Drain the tofu, wrap it in a cloth and gently press it out.

2. Meanwhile, core, seed and cut the peppers into 3 cm/1¼ inch dice. Seed and finely chop the green chilli. Finely chop the garlic and onions.

3. Preheat the wok, add the pine nuts and dry-fry, stirring constantly, for about 30–60 seconds, until golden. Remove the pine nuts and set aside. Heat the oil in the wok until it is smoking. Cut the tofu into 3 cm/1¼ inch cubes. Add the tofu to the wok and stir-fry until browned all over. Remove the tofu and set aside.

4. Add the diced peppers, chilli, garlic and onions and stir-fry for 1–2 minutes, until the onions are translucent. Pour in the soy sauce, rice wine or sherry and the vegetable stock. Return the tofu cubes to the wok and braise for about 5 minutes.

5. Mix together the cornflour and the water to make a smooth paste. Add to the wok and cook, stirring constantly, until the sauce has thickened. Transfer to a warm serving dish, scatter over the pine nuts and serve immediately with boiled rice.

Above: Sesame-coated tofu with mushrooms
Below: Tofu with peppers

Tofu with sugar-snap peas and chillies

Good value

Serves 4
6 dried shiitake mushrooms
120 ml/4 fl oz lukewarm water
500 g/1¼ lb tofu
4 spring onions
3 garlic cloves
1 small fresh green chilli
2 dried chillies
60 ml/4 tablespoons soy oil
200 g/7 oz sugar-snap peas or mangetouts
120 ml/4 fl oz vegetable stock
30–45 ml/2–3 tablespoons dark soy sauce
sugar
10 ml/2 teaspoons cornflour
45 ml/3 tablespoons water
salt
boiled rice, to serve

Approximately per portion:
1,900 kj/450 kcal
20 g protein
33 g fat
18 g carbohydrate

- Soaking time: about 1 hour

- Approximate preparation time: 25 minutes

1. Soak the mushrooms in the warm water for about 1 hour. Drain the tofu. Put a weighted board on top of it and leave for about 30 minutes.

2. Meanwhile, thinly slice the spring onions. Finely chop the garlic. Seed and finely chop the fresh chilli. Crush the dried chillies in a mortar with a pestle or in a spice grinder.

3. Drain the mushrooms and reserve the soaking water. Cut off and discard the stalks and cut the caps into quarters. Pat the tofu dry and cut each block into 8 cubes

4. Heat the oil in a preheated wok. Add the mushrooms, spring onions, garlic, chillies and sugar-snap peas or mangetouts and stir-fry until the onions are translucent. Add the tofu cubes and stir-fry briefly. Then pour in the mushroom soaking liquid and the vegetable stock. Add the soy sauce and a pinch of sugar and simmer for about 5 minutes.

5. Stir together the cornflour and water to make a smooth paste. Stir the cornflour mixture into the wok and cook, stirring constantly, until the sauce has thickened. Taste and if necessary, season with salt. Serve immediately with boiled rice.

Tofu with beansprouts and cucumber

For beginners

Serves 4
500 g/1¼ lb tofu
1 cucumber
salt
200 g/7 oz beansprouts
½ bunch chives
30 ml/2 tablespoons sesame seeds
60 ml/4 tablespoons groundnut or soy oil
120 ml/4 fl oz vegetable stock
30 ml/2 tablespoons peanut butter
freshly ground black pepper

Approximately per portion:
2,200 kj/520 kcal
23 g protein
43 g fat
10 g carbohydrate

- Approximate preparation time: 40 minutes

1. Drain the tofu. Put a weighted board on top of it and leave for about 30 minutes. Peel the cucumber and halve it lengthways. Seed and cut into 2 cm/¾ inch wide strips. Add a little salt and leave it to dégorge for about 10 minutes. Then drain.

2. Rinse the beansprouts. Finely chop the chives. Pat the tofu dry and cut each block into 8 cubes.

3. Preheat a wok, add the sesame seeds and dry-fry, stirring constantly, until they give off an aroma. Remove from the wok and set aside. Return the wok to the heat and heat the oil. Add the tofu and stir-fry until brown all over.

4. Add the cucumber, beansprouts and vegetable stock to the wok and simmer over a low heat for 5 minutes. Stir in the peanut butter and season to taste with salt and pepper. Transfer to a dish, scatter over the sesame seeds and serve.

Above: Tofu with sugar-snap peas and chillies
Below: Tofu with beansprouts and cucumber

Vegetable rice

For beginners

Serves 4
25 g/1 oz wood ear mushrooms
400 ml/14 fl oz vegetable stock
200 g/7 oz long grain rice
2 red peppers
1 onion
1 garlic clove
2 spring onions or 1 leek
2 beef tomatoes
1 bunch fresh flat leaf parsley
30 ml/2 tablespoons olive oil
25 g/1 oz butter
salt
cayenne pepper

Approximately per portion:
2,400 kj/570 kcal
32 g protein
26 g fat
59 g carbohydrate

● Approximate preparation
time: 35 minutes

1. Soak the mushrooms in warm water for 20 minutes. Drain and rinse the mushrooms. Remove and discard the hard stalks and cut the caps into 1 cm/½ inch strips.

2. Bring the vegetable stock to the boil in a saucepan. Add the rice and bring back to the boil. Lower the heat, cover and cook for about 20 minutes, until the rice is tender and has absorbed all the liquid.

3. Meanwhile, core and seed the red peppers and cut the flesh into small diamond shapes. Finely chop the onion and garlic. Thinly slice

the spring onions or the white part of the leek, diagonally.

4. Blanch the tomatoes in boiling water for 1–2 minutes. Skin, seed and dice the flesh. Pull the parsley leaves off the stems and finely chop them.

5. Heat the olive oil and butter in a preheated wok. Add the peppers, onion, garlic and spring onions or leek and stir-fry until the onion is translucent. Push the vegetables to one side, add the rice and stir-fry for 2–3 minutes.

6. Quickly mix together the rice and vegetables in the wok and stir in the mushrooms, tomatoes and parsley. Season to taste with salt and a pinch of cayenne pepper and serve immediately.

Pilaff with almonds

Good value

Serves 4
50 g/2 oz seedless raisins
500 ml/17 fl oz vegetable stock
250 g/9 oz long grain rice
4 shallots
2 garlic cloves
1 small fresh red chilli
4 small yellow peppers
1 bunch fresh mixed herbs
50 g/2 oz chopped almonds
50 g/2 oz pine nuts
45 ml/3 tablespoons olive oil
25 g/1 oz butter
20 g/¾ oz frozen peas, thawed
salt
curry powder

Approximately per portion:
3,400 kj/810 kcal
42 g protein
40 g fat
76 g carbohydrate

● Approximate preparation
time: 35 minutes

1. Put the raisins in a bowl and pour in sufficient hot water to cover and set aside. Put the vegetable stock and rice in a large saucepan and bring to the boil. Cover, lower the heat and simmer for 25 minutes, until the rice is tender and all the liquid has been completely absorbed.

2. Dice the shallots, garlic and fresh red chilli.

3. Core and seed the peppers and cut the flesh into thin strips. Finely chop the herbs.

4. Preheat the wok. Add the almonds and pine nuts and dry-fry, stirring constantly, until golden. Remove the nuts from the wok. Heat the oil and butter in the wok. Add the peas, shallots, garlic, chilli and peppers and stir-fry for about 2 minutes. Push them to one side of the wok, add the rice and stir-fry for 2 minutes.

5. Drain the raisins and stir them into the wok, together with the almonds, pine nuts and herbs. Season to taste with salt and curry powder and serve immediately.

Above: Pilaff with almonds
Below: Vegetable rice

Spring rolls

Easy to make

Serves 4
10 g/¼ oz wood ear mushrooms
115 g/4 oz beansprouts
4 spring onions
2 heads celery
2 medium carrots
150 g/5 oz tofu
1 garlic clove
30 ml/2 tablespoons Chinese rice
   wine or dry sherry
30 ml/2 tablespoons soy sauce
5 ml/1 teaspoon cornflour
1 dried chilli
24 spring roll skins
500 ml/17 fl oz groundnut or soy oil
salt

Approximately per portion:
2,300 kj/ 550 kcal
6 g protein
52 g fat
11 g carbohydrate

● Approximate preparation
  time: 40 minutes

1. Put the wood ear mushrooms in a bowl, cover with warm water and set aside to soak for about 20 minutes. Then drain and reserve 30 ml/2 tablespoons of the soaking water. Cut off and discard the hard stalks and cut the caps into thin strips.

2. Wash the beansprouts and drain well.

3. Cut the spring onions, celery and carrots into thin strips about 4 cm/1½ inches long.

4. Drain the tofu, press it lightly under a cloth, then roughly crumble with a fork. Crush the garlic. Mix together the Chinese rice wine or sherry, soy sauce, reserved mushroom soaking water and the cornflour. Grind the chilli in a mortar with a pestle or in a spice grinder.

5. Soak the spring roll skins briefly in cold water to make them supple. Then spread them out in pairs, one on top of the other, on a damp tea cloth. Cover them with another damp teacloth.

Tip

Serve the spring rolls as a starter or part of a menu. Put small bowls of soy sauce and other Asian sauces on the table as dipping sauces.

You can buy spring roll skins in Chinese food shops or in large supermarkets with a good selection of Asian products.

6. Heat 30 ml/2 tablespoons of the oil in a preheated wok. Add the onions, celery, carrots and beansprouts and stir-fry for about 30 seconds. Add the crumbled tofu, mushrooms and garlic and stir-fry for a further 2 minutes. Stir in the chilli and the rice wine mixture and bring to the boil.

Variation
Non-vegetarians can substitute finely minced chicken breast or beef for the tofu.

7. Season to taste with salt, remove the wok from the heat and set aside to cool slightly. Then divide the mixture between he spring roll skins. Fold in the sides of the skins, then roll them up from bottom to top.

8. Wipe the wok with kitchen paper and return to the heat. Heat the remaining oil until it is smoking. Add the spring rolls, 4 at a time, and stir-fry for 2–3 minutes until they are crispy brown. Drain on kitchen paper, while you cook the remainder. Serve hot.

Spicy cabbage with cashew nuts

Good value

This dish originated in the vegetarian cuisine of India, but there it is much more hotly spiced.

Serves 4
1 medium Savoy cabbage (about
    800 g/1¾ lb)
2 dried chillies
5 ml/1 teaspoon yellow
    mustard seeds
1 small bay leaf
50 g/2 oz clarified butter
115 g/4 oz shelled cashew nuts
2.5 ml/½ teaspoon ground ginger
120 ml/4 fl oz vegetable stock
300 g/11 oz frozen peas, thawed
15 ml/1 tablespoon curry powder
salt
sugar
30–45 ml/2–3 tablespoons full-
    fat yogurt
boiled rice, to serve

Approximately per portion:
1,800 kj/430 kcal
23 g protein
27 g fat
26 g carbohydrate

● Approximate preparation
   time: 35 minutes

1. Remove the outer leaves and stem from the cabbage and shred the leaves into 2 cm/¾ inch strips.

2. Pound together the chillies, mustard seeds and bay leaf in a mortar with a pestle or work in a food processor. Heat the clarified butter in a preheated wok. Add the cashew nuts and stir-fry until they are golden. Remove the nuts from the wok and set aside. Add the ground spices and the ginger to the wok and stir-fry for about 1 minute.

3. Add the cabbage and stir-fry until it has wilted. Add the vegetable stock and the peas, cover and braise for about 8 minutes.

4. Stir in the curry powder and season to taste with salt and sugar. Cook for a further 5 minutes over a medium heat to allow the liquid to reduce.

5. Stir in the yogurt and cashew nuts. Transfer to a warmed serving dish and serve immediately with boiled rice.

Mushroom and celery stir-fry

Quick to make

Serves 4
400 g/14 oz straw mushrooms
250 g/9 oz shiitake mushrooms
400 g/14 oz chestnut or large
    white mushrooms
4 heads celery
2 onions
½ bunch flat leaf parsley
40 g/1½ oz clarified butter
60 ml/4 tablespoons dry white wine
60 ml/4 tablespoons crème fraîche
salt
freshly ground white pepper
2.5 ml/½ teaspoon ground coriander
boiled noodles, to serve

Approximately per portion:
1,200 kj/290 kcal
9 g protein
21 g fat
8 g carbohydrate

● Approximate preparation
   time: 25 minutes

1. Remove and discard any hard stalks from the mushrooms and cut all the mushrooms into very thin slices.

2. Cut the celery into 2 cm/¾ inch slices. Finely chop the onions. Pull the parsley leaves off the stems and chop finely.

3. Heat the clarified butter in a preheated wok. Add the onions and stir-fry until they are translucent. Add the mushrooms and celery and stir-fry for about 1 minute.

4. Pour in the wine and cook, stirring constantly, for about 3 minutes. Add the crème fraîche, season to taste with salt and pepper and stir in the coriander. Transfer to a serving dish, sprinkle over the parsley and serve with boiled noodles.

Above: Spicy cabbage with cashew nuts
Below: Mushroom and celery stir-fry

Green vegetable curry

Rather time-consuming

Serves 4–6
250 g/9 oz young green beans
2 green peppers
4 yellow peppers
1 fresh green chilli
1 bunch spring onions
4 young carrots
3 garlic cloves
3 cm/1¼ inch piece fresh
   root ginger
75 ml/5 tablespoons groundnut or
   soy oil
5 ml/1 teaspoon pale mustard seeds
5 ml/1 teaspoon ground coriander
250 g/9 oz sugar-snap peas
115 g/4 oz desiccated coconut
250 ml/8 fl oz vegetable stock
salt
5 ml/1 teaspoon sugar
150 ml/¼ pint full-fat yogurt
15–30 ml/1–2 tablespoons curry
   powder
boiled rice, to serve

For 6 people, approximately per portion:
1,700 kj/400 kcal
15 g protein
28 g fat
26 g carbohydrate

● Approximate preparation
   time: 45 minutes

1. Break any large green beans in half. Core and seed the green and yellow peppers and cut the flesh into thin strips. Seed the green chilli and chop very finely.

2. Finely chop the white parts of the spring onions and thinly slice the green parts diagonally. Finely chop the carrots. Chop the garlic and ginger.

3. Heat the oil in a preheated wok. Add the ginger, garlic, mustard seeds and coriander and stir-fry over a medium heat for about 1 minute. Do not allow the garlic to turn brown or it will become bitter and inedible.

4. Add the beans and stir-fry for about 30 seconds. Push to one side, add the sugar-snap peas and stir-fry for 30 seconds. Push to one side, add the peppers and chilli and stir-fry for 30 seconds. Push to one side, add the spring onions and stir-fry for 30 seconds. Push to one side, add the carrots and stir-fry for 30 seconds.

5. Stir in the coconut, then pour in the vegetable stock.

6. Cook the vegetables, stirring constantly, for about 6–8 minutes, until tender, but still firm to the bite. Season to taste with salt and stir in sugar.

7. Remove the wok from the heat and stir in the yogurt and curry powder. Serve with boiled rice.

In appealing shades of green, this vegetable curry not only looks beautiful, but also tastes delicious.

Pak choi with prawns

Easy to make

Pak choi, also known as bok choi, is a Chinese variety of cabbage, which is now commercially cultivated in Europe.

Serves 4
400 g/14 oz peeled, cooked prawns
1 egg white
15 ml/1 tablespoon cornflour
freshly ground black pepper
1 large or 2 small heads pak choi
*   (about 600 g/1 lb 5 oz)*
1 onion
1 garlic clove
60 ml/4 tablespoons groundnut or
*   soy oil*
120 ml/4 fl oz vegetable stock
60 ml/4 tablespoons dry white wine
salt
ground ginger

Approximately per portion:
1,900 kj/450 kcal
29 g protein
29 g fat
15 g carbohydrate

● Approximate preparation
   time: 30 minutes

1. Devein the prawns. Beat the egg white until soft peaks form, then mix it with the cornflour. Season the prawns with pepper and mix them with the egg white.

2. Cut the pak choi stalks, so that the leaves fall loosely apart. Remove and coarsely chop the green leaves. Cut the stalks in half lengthways, then in half across. Finely chop the onion and garlic.

3. Heat 30 ml/2 tablespoons oil in a preheated wok. Add the pak choi stalks and stir-fry for about 2 minutes. Add 30 ml/ 2 tablespoons of the stock and 30 ml/2 tablespoons of the wine and cook for a further 5 minutes. Remove the stalks from the wok and set aside.

4. Heat the remaining oil in the wok until it is smoking. Add the onion and garlic and stir-fry until they are translucent. Add the prawns and stir-fry for a further 2 minutes. Pour in the remaining stock and the remaining wine. Add the pak choi leaves, return the stalks to the wok and bring to the boil. Season to taste with salt and ginger and serve immediately.

Beans with bamboo shoots

For beginners

Serves 4
1 kg/2¼ lb broad beans
250 g/ 9 oz young green beans
250 g/9 oz can bamboo shoots
30 ml/2 tablespoons olive oil
20 g/¾ oz clarified butter
250 ml/8 fl oz vegetable stock
5 ml/1 teaspoon cornflour
salt
freshly ground white pepper

Approximately per portion:
1,600 kj/380 kcal
24 g protein
21 g fat
26 g carbohydrate

● Approximate preparation
  time: 35 minutes

1. Shell the broad beans and blanch them in boiling water for about 3 minutes. Drain, refresh in cold water and remove the skins.

2. Break any large green beans in half. Drain the bamboo shoots and cut them with a serrated knife into strips about 5 mm/¼ inch thick, 2 cm/¾ inch wide and 3 cm/1¼ inches long.

3. Heat the oil and clarified butter in a preheated wok. Add the broad beans, green beans and bamboo shoots and stir-fry for 2 minutes. Reserve 30 ml/ 2 tablespoons of the stock and pour the remainder into the wok. Cover and cook for about 5 minutes.

4. Mix together the cornflour and reserved stock to make a smooth paste. Stir the cornflour paste into the wok and cook, stirring constantly, until thickened. Season to taste with salt and pepper. Transfer to a serving dish and serve immediately.

Straw mushrooms with celery

Easy to make

You can serve this dish as a vegetable accompaniment to poached fish or white meat or serve on its own in a meal with several courses.

Serves 4
500 g/1¼ lb straw mushrooms
2 heads celery
4 spring onions
115 g/4 oz cherry tomatoes
60 ml/4 tablespoons olive oil
60 ml/4 tablespoons dry white wine
salt
freshly ground white pepper
5–10 ml/1–2 teaspoons balsamic
  vinegar
sugar

Approximately per portion:
1,200 kj/290 kcal
3 g protein
25 g fat
4 g carbohydrate

● Approximate preparation
  time: 35 minutes

---

1. According to their size, leave the mushrooms whole or cut them into halves or quarters.

2. Cut off the celery leaves, chop coarsely and set aside. Cut the sticks into 2 cm/¾ inch thick slices.

3. Thinly slice the spring onions diagonally. Cut the cherry tomatoes in half.

4. Heat the oil in a preheated wok. Add the mushrooms, celery and spring onions and stir-fry for about 2 minutes. Pour in the wine and cook, stirring frequently, until nearly all the liquid has evaporated. Season to taste with salt, pepper, vinegar and sugar.

5. Add the cherry tomatoes and heat through. Transfer to warm serving dish, scatter the celery greenery over the vegetables and serve immediately.

Brussels sprouts with apples

Unusual

Serves 4
800 g/1¾ lb Brussels sprouts
75 g/3 oz butter
120 ml/4 fl oz vegetable stock
500 g/1¼ lb tart apples
2.5 ml/½ teaspoon ground coriander
5 ml/1 teaspoon sesame seeds
90 ml/6 tablespoons dry
  white wine
salt
freshly ground white pepper
sugar

Approximately per portion:
1,500 kj/360 kcal
18 g protein
21 g fat
21 g carbohydrate

● Approximate preparation
  time: 35 minutes

---

1. Cut crosses into the ends of the Brussels sprouts' stalks.

2. Melt 25 g/1 oz of the butter in a preheated wok. Add the Brussels sprouts and stir-fry for 2–3 minutes. Pour in the vegetable stock, cover and cook for 15 minutes, until tender but still firm to the bite.

3. Peel the apples, quarter and core them. Then cut the quarters in half crossways.

4. Drain the Brussels sprouts, set aside and keep warm. Wipe the wok with kitchen paper and return to the heat. Melt the remaining butter in the wok. Add the coriander and sesame seeds and stir-fry for about 1 minute.

5. Add the apples and stir-fry for 1 further minute. Pour in the white wine, cover and cook for about 5 minutes.

6. Return the Brussels sprouts to the wok and gently heat through over a low heat, stirring constantly, for about 1 minute. Season to taste with salt, pepper and sugar. Transfer to a warm serving dish and serve immediately.

Above: Straw mushrooms with celery
Below: Brussels sprouts with apples

Great Little Cook Books
Wok Cooking

Published originally under the title
Aus dem Wok by Gräfe und Unzer
Verlag GmbH, München

© 1992 by Gräfe und Unzer Verlag
GmbH, München

English-language edition
© 1998 by Transedition Limited,
Oxford, England

This edition published in 2001
by Advanced Marketing,
Bicester, Oxfordshire.

Translation:
Translate-A-Book, Oxford

Editing:
Linda Doeser

Typesetting:
Organ Graphic, Abingdon

10 9 8 7 6 5 4 3 2
Printed in Dubai

ISBN 1 901683 16 8

Note:
Quantities for all recipes are given
in both metric and imperial
measures and, if appropriate, in
standard measuring spoons. They
are not interchangeable, so readers
should follow one set or the other.
5 ml = 1 teaspoon
15 ml = 1 tablespoon

Veronika Müller
is a professional home economist
and journalist. At present, she lives
in the most beautiful corner of
Baden, Ortenau in Germany. She
has worked for 20 years as a
freelance food journalist and writes
books and articles on nutrition and
creates recipes for newspapers.

Odette Teubner
was taught by her father, the
internationally renowned food
photographer, Christian Teubner.
She then worked for some months
as a fashion photographer. At
present she works exclusively in
the Teubner Studio for Food
Photography. In her spare time she
is an enthusiastic painter of
children's portraits. She uses her
own son as a model.

Kerstin Mosny
studied photography at a college in
French-speaking Switzerland. After
that she worked as an assistant to
various photographers, including
the food photographer, Jürgen
Tapprich in Zürich. She now works
in the Teubner Studio.